Let's Get Comfortable

Being

Uncomfortable

How To Break Free From Your Fear Zone

Chris Packham

Let's Get Comfortable Being Uncomfortable
How To Break Free From Your Fear Zone

Copyright ©2025 Chris Packham

ISBN: 978-1-61170-333-7

Photo from Family Collection.

Published in 2025 by Robertson Publishing
Book printed in the USA and UK on acid-free paper.

Acknowledgment

I want to give special thanks to my Lord and provider, Jesus Christ the great I Am for giving me the strength to keep moving forward each day, for surrounding me with the right people, and for carrying me through every difficult moment.

Grandpa

To Grandpa Craig, whose inspiring stories taught me to dream big and believe in myself. Thank you for taking the time to show me what it truly means to be a gentleman. I love you, Grandpa Craig.

Blanca

To a strong, beautiful, and compassionate woman who never gave up on me my best friend in life, always by my side, listening without judgment and offering guidance when I needed it most. To my incredible children, James, Diamond, and Titan you are my world, my purpose, and my daily inspiration. And to my son-in-law, Mario, thank you for your patience, kindness, and the love you showed my daughter.

Contents:

1. Introduction   1

2. The thief in your hands   7

3. The clockmaker's gift   11

4. The mask of delay   13

5. Becoming your own flame   17

6. The spark that starts within   20

7. Rising in the face of resistance   22

8. W.H.Y   25

9. Learning to walk in your new skin   28

10. Your thoughts create your world   32

11. The war inside the mirror   37

12. Roots that withstand the storm   41

13. Clearing the fog   44

14. Embracing the unseen path   46

15. Self-Rating Anxious Scale   49

16. Daily rituals of self-love   57

17. When words listen back   62

18. Dancing with discomfort   66

19. Shedding the masks   74

20. The fire that belongs only to you   76

21. The strength between storms   80

22. Live Now   84

23. Notes   88

24. About the author   89

Introduction:

Let's Get Comfortable Being Uncomfortable is more than a motivational book it's a mirror held up to your soul, forcing you to confront the places you've hidden from yourself. It strips away the illusion that growth is supposed to feel easy and replaces it with the truth: every breakthrough begins where comfort ends. Within its pages, you'll find stories that shake you awake, reflections that pierce through excuses, and wisdom that challenges the very foundation of your fears. It doesn't promise a gentle journey, it promises a transformative one. This book speaks to the warrior inside you, the part that knows you were made for more, even when life tries to convince you otherwise. It teaches you to find peace in uncertainty, purpose in pain, and strength in vulnerability. Let's Get Comfortable Being Uncomfortable isn't a guide you read once it's a manifesto you live by, one that dares you to stop running from discomfort and start walking straight through it toward your destiny.

I just finished the weekend teaching a Mix Martial Arts workshop in Las Vegas, Nevada and needed to pick up my ticket to return back to San Jose, California. After arriving at the airport, I went to the front counter to pick up my ticket. As I started walking towards the gate I notice more than a few people standing around as this man was telling everyone their age and where they were traveling to. This man grabbed my interest in how he was doing this, so I stood in line to wait my turn. I was next, I walk up to him, and he says, "You are 28 years old, and you are traveling to San Jose, California." I said, "That is correct, how did you do that"? The man smiled and the next person stepped up to get his reading. I walked away and said to myself this is some kind of trick and wanted to know how he was doing that, so I waited for about 10 minutes and then went right back in line to get another turn. I step up to the man, and he said, "You are still 28 years old heading back to San Jose, California." At that point I was shocked, so I walked away once more watching him guess everyone's age and where they were traveling. This man never missed a beat and at this point I was so intrigued how in the world this man was getting everyone right. I can be a real stubborn man, so I waited for another 20 minutes before getting back in the line. I step up for the third time, and the man said, "You are still 28 years old, and you have just missed your flight to San Jose, California."

<u>Moral of the Story:</u>

Sometimes, our curiosity and stubbornness to understand *how* something works can distract us from *what truly matters*. In chasing answers, we can lose sight of the moment right in front of us, the opportunity, the flight, the lesson. Life isn't always about figuring everything out; it's about knowing when to move forward and trusting the journey before time passes you by. Sometimes the wisest thing we can do is take the next step, even when we don't have all the answers.

This book is written to suggest techniques and strategies, inspire you and motivate you to new heights. To help invest in you, and to give you clear vision. Just like when you get a new pair of glasses you have a clear vision of what you are looking at or a clear vision of your world. Throughout most of my life, I spent little time pondering who I am, what's my value, my purpose. It only seems apparent that there were many problems with myself, more than likely caused by my family or my environment. Even at this moment in my life I try to pinpoint who I am and what my purpose is. When you live your life based on sentiments, trying not to hurt everyone's feelings or doing things just because it feels good to do it, you'll get nowhere twice as fast. I was the award-winning people pleaser. I try not to live by tradition either. If you do the same things the same way you have always done them, you will continue to get the same outcome. For many years now, I have wanted to write a book on motivation. You can't read the label when you are locked in the box. Don't allow Mr. fear or as I like to call it "our itty-bitty shitty committee,"

As you read through this book, I'm going to ask for your participation. You are probably wondering how one participates in a reading book. I'm glad you asked. When you are reading and I'm telling a story or explaining, and you come across "Fair enough." I would like you to repeat after me in the same words, however out loud. The theory behind this is to start re-training your brain for the positive.

(Law of Forgetting)

Originally developed by Hermann Ebbinghaus in the late 19th century, this describes how memory decays over time if you don't try to retain or review the information.

Time After Learning:

Within one hour of learning, you forget about **56%** of the information. After **24 hours**, roughly **67%** is forgotten. By **30 days**, as much as **86%** of what you learned fades from memory.

(Law of remembering)

Recently: We remember best what we heard last.
Frequently: We remember what we hear most often.

Impact: We remember most of the things that are presented dramatically.

Application: We remember most of the things we have use for.

Notes:

_____

_____

_____

_____

_____

_____

_____

_____

_____

_____

_____

_____

_____

The mountain within:

Blanca had always avoided challenges that made her heart race. Heights, crowds, even trying something new they all felt like walls she couldn't climb. Yet when her company organized a team-building hike to a cliffside viewpoint, something inside her stirred: a quiet whisper that maybe fear was a signal, not a stop sign. The climb was harder than she imagined. Every shaky step and quivering breath tested her resolve. Halfway up, she wanted to turn back, but then she noticed the small flowers clinging to the rocks, surviving despite the wind and the height. Inspired, she pressed on. When she finally reached the summit, the vast valley stretched beneath her, golden in the late afternoon sun. She realized the mountain she had truly climbed wasn't the cliff, it was her own doubt.

Moral of the story:

The greatest mountains are often the fears we carry inside us. Facing them teaches us that courage isn't the absence of fear, it's moving forward anyway. Can I get a "Fair enough."

If this book serves its purpose, you will encounter a thought or perhaps several that resonates deep within your heart and soul. When that happens, I hope it sparks action, urging you to move past the challenges, barriers, and struggles that stand in your way today. Life is always in motion. It rarely stays the same and often surprises us, sometimes in ways we'd rather avoid. Think of Murphy's Law: *"Anything that can go wrong, will go wrong."* It's a stark reminder that life isn't a straight path. It's a blend of highs and lows, joy and sorrow, triumphs and setbacks. The choice is yours: either you take charge of the day, or the day takes charge of you.

Now, if life were truly fair, teachers would be paid a million dollars per year, and athletes would be paid in tips. But that's not the reality we've been handed. Since we can't rewrite the rules, the next best choice is to practice acceptance. Embracing life as it isn't weakness its strength. It's the power to see things clearly and still choose to move forward. When you truly accept what comes, the chaos feels more manageable, and the weight on your shoulders begins to lift. Say this aloud with conviction: *No matter how hard it gets, no matter how rough it feels, I am going to make it.* And remember: the very first step toward a meaningful life is to stop killing time and start truly living.

<u>Notes:</u>

_____

_____

_____

_____

_____

_____

_____

_____

_____

_____

_____

_____

The thief in your hands:

An athlete won't judge you for working out; A millionaire won't judge you for starting a business; A musician won't judge you for trying to sing a song. It's always the people going nowhere that have something to say. Start living for YOU and **stop killing time!**

In 1998, I unlocked the door to my very first martial arts school, **Packham's Kenpo Karate**. Back then, I was proud to stand among members of the American Kenpo Karate Association and other Kenpo organizations, training under the guidance of Richard Willetts.

That same year, Mr. Willetts and eight other school owners signed up for a workshop led by no one other than Tony Robbins *Awaken the Giant Within*. By pure grace and a stroke of luck, I found myself there too. Meeting Tony wasn't just an introduction it was a jolt to the soul. His energy didn't just fill the room, it shook it. His voice thundered with conviction, and I remember the crowd erupting with the kind of electricity you feel when your team clinches the championship overtime. That day taught me a truth I've never forgotten life's too short to sit on the sidelines. **Stop killing time.**

Time is our most valuable currency finite, fragile, and impossible to replace. We're given it not to drift but to build, to dream, to become. And here's the beautiful paradox: we can only connect life's dots by looking back, but it's faith that drives us forward trusting the pieces will someday make sense.

Yet, the clock keeps moving. The bar of our lives shortened with each sunrise, and no amount of money or wishful thinking can stretch it. The real loss isn't time itself, it's

7

wasting it. We major in minor things. A five-minute issue becomes a five-hour distraction. Hours turn into days, days into months, and before we know it, five years have slipped through our fingers like sand.

So let that truth settle in deep. The clock is always ticking, and the decision is always yours: will you waste the time you've been given or finally use it to live?

Our lifespan is a mystery. Being human is both a gift and a burden, a double-edged sword. Too often, we deceive ourselves into thinking we have unlimited time to accomplish what matters, and in doing so, we squander the precious hours we've been given.

We all aspire to shine, to become that diamond in the sky. But diamonds are only formed under pressure. In the same way, we must create a sense of urgency within ourselves to truly understand the value of time. Otherwise, one day we will wake up, look in the mirror, and whisper the most haunting question of all: *Where did the time go?*

Every challenge you face is an opportunity to grow stronger. Remember, to make time work for you the five C's are more than principles, they're a way of showing up in life.

Clear: Clarity is confidence in motion. When you speak or act with clarity, you remove confusion not just for others, but for yourself. It means knowing your "why" and letting it guide every word and decision.

Concise: Time is precious, and attention is fleeting. Say what matters and say it with impact. The fewer the words, the stronger the message because truth doesn't need decoration.

Compelling: This is where heart meets purpose. A compelling message moves people because it's real. Its passion wrapped in authenticity, a voice that connects instead of impresses.

Committed: Commitment separates dreamers from doers. It's the promise you keep to yourself when no one's watching, the fire that keeps burning when motivation fades.

Consistent: Consistency is where trust is born. It's showing up again and again until your actions echo louder than your words. It's the quiet rhythm behind every success story.

Master the five C's, and you don't just communicate you lead, inspire, and leave a mark.

Those things you keep postponing with the phrase, *"someday I'll get to it,"* are quietly stealing your destiny. Because *someday* is not a day it's a dead end. And its final destination is a small town called **Nowhere.** Can I get a "Fair enough."

You think it is too late. You look around and see others ahead of you. You start to believe you have missed your chance. But, let me tell you something you haven't. Time doesn't run out when you fail. It only runs out when you stop trying. Every breath you take is another opportunity. Every sunrise is an invitation to start again. Keep Going.

Let's get comfortable being uncomfortable

Notes:

_____

_____

_____

_____

_____

_____

_____

_____

_____

_____

_____

_____

The clockmaker's gift:

In a small mountain village, there lived an old clockmaker named Michael. His shop sat at the heart of the town square, filled with hundreds of ticking clocks, all clocks, pocket watches, sun dials, and even one made from the bones of an ancient tree. People came from far and wide to have Michael repair their broken timepieces, because they said no one understood the way he did. One day, a young man named Nico came rushing into Michael's shop. His hair was uncombed, his eyes restless, his mind cluttered. "Master Michael," he said breathlessly, "I need your help. My days are slipping through my fingers. I wake up early and sleep late, yet nothing gets done. My dreams are fading into dust."

Tao smiled softly, motioning to the hundreds of clocks that surrounded them. "Which clock would you like me to fix?" "But I didn't bring a clock," Nico said, confused. The old man chuckled. "Ah, but you did. You brought me the most important one your life's clock."

He handed Nico a small, broken pocket watch and said, "Take this. Every morning, wind it once. Every hour, when you hear it tick, ask yourself one question: Am I spending this hour or wasting it?" Nico left the shop puzzled, but he did as he was told. On the first day, he realized how much time he spent reacting checking his messages, worrying about things that hadn't happened, saying "yes" to things that didn't matter. The ticking reminded him to choose differently. On the second day, he learned to prioritize finishing what mattered first before tending to what was merely urgent. On the third day, he began to notice the rhythm of his life how productivity wasn't about doing more, but about doing what mattered most with intention.

Days turned to weeks, weeks to months. The ticking of the clock became a teacher. He began to wake not with dread, but with direction. His life no longer felt like a race it felt like a song with meaning between every note. One morning, he returned to the clockmaker's shop. "Master Michael," he said with a smile, "I've fixed my time."

Michael nodded knowingly. "You didn't fix time, my boy. You learned to master yourself within it." As Nico turned to leave, Michael called out, "Remember, time is not something you find it's something you make. And every tick of the clock is a chance to begin again."

Moral of the Story:

Time management is not about controlling the clock it's about aligning your purpose with your priorities. You can't conquer time until you first conquer distraction, indecision, and fear. The wisest use of time is to spend it on what outlives you. Can I get a "Fair enough."

Notes:

_____

_____

_____

_____

_____

_____

_____

The mask of delay:

For a long time, procrastination was my game. I didn't call it that back then I just thought I was pacing myself, giving myself "plenty of time." But looking back, I see it clearly: my poor time management was rooted in putting things off, especially when it came to training.

I remember telling myself, *"I've got sixteen weeks before my fight in Japan."* That sounded like forever. Sure, I trained, but it wasn't at my full potential. I gave about fifty percent when I knew I had one hundred and ten in me. And the question that haunted me was: *Why do I keep doing this to myself? Why settle for half-effort when I know I'm capable of more?*

Eventually, I had to face the truth. If I wanted real results in the ring and in life I needed to stop procrastinating and start owning my time. That meant looking honestly at where my hours were slipping away, cutting out the timewasters, and paying attention to when my energy was at its peak. Because time management isn't just about calendars and to do lists it's about aligning your effort with your purpose.

True management of time starts with clarity: defining your goals, setting your priorities, and creating a plan of action that fits into your life. And once you know what matters most, the real test is learning to do *that* first. Because procrastination is always waiting, tempting you to delay what needs to be done today for some undefined "later."

Here's the truth: procrastination has no reason, no logic. It simply feeds on hesitation. And when left unchecked, it becomes dangerous not just to your schedule, but to your dreams, your goals, your talents, and even your livelihood.

There once was a man named Chris, a gifted painter whose art could move even the most hardened hearts. People said his brush did not paint it breathed. Each stroke whispered of life, of dreams, of something divine that could not be spoken in words. But Chris had the habit of a small, invisible chain that bound him tighter than any prison could. He would say, "Tomorrow, I'll begin my masterpiece."

Each morning, he rose with grand intentions. He prepared his brushes, laid out his paints, and stood before the blank canvas. But then he'd tell himself, "I'll start after I eat. "Then after a walk. Then after the sun sets the lighting would be better then. And so, the days slipped by, like sand between careless fingers. Seasons turned. The world outside his studio changed leaves fell, snow came, flowers returned. Yet the great white canvas stood untouched.

Chris grew old. His hands began to tremble. His once bright eyes dimmed. Still, he whispered, "Tomorrow. I'll start tomorrow." Then, one cold morning, his heart faithful and patient until that day refused to wait any longer. When the villagers found him, the easel still stood in the corner, the paints untouched, the brushes clean. At his funeral, a young boy one who had often watched Chris through the window asked, "What was he waiting for?" The village elder sighed. "He was waiting for the perfect moment," he said. "But life only gives us this one the imperfect one we're living right now."

Years later, that same boy became a painter. He kept one blank canvas in his studio as a reminder. Above it, he painted in gold letters: **"Tomorrow is a thief that steals your dreams and calls it patience."**

Moral of the Story:

Procrastination is the silent assassin of greatness. The perfect moment will never come, only the present moment will. Dreams die not because we lack time, but because we keep believing we'll have more of it.

That's where hope comes in. HOPE can mean **Hang On, Pain Ends.** It can also mean **"Have Only Positive Expectations."** Either way, it's a reminder that change is possible if you refuse to quit.

Here's my challenge to you **commit the next 90 days to giving 110% of yourself.** No shortcuts. No excuses. Every day, focus on improving by just **1%.** That's it one small step forward, one intentional choice, one moment of discipline over distraction.

At the end of those 90 days, pause and take inventory. Has procrastination loosened its grip, or have you fed it more power? If you've improved even slightly you've proven something far more powerful than perfection: that **change lives within your control.**

And if your results aren't what you hoped for, that's okay. You'll still stand at a crossroads the same choice you've always had to fall back into comfort or rise again with clarity and conviction. But here's what I know: once you've tasted progress, once you've felt that spark of growth, going backward won't feel the same. Because you'll have glimpsed what's possible and that vision is impossible to forget.

You have to believe that you were meant to stand out, because you fly like an eagle and don't play with the turkeys on the bottom, because the bottom is overcrowded. Can I get a "Fair enough."

<u>Notes:</u>

_____

_____

_____

_____

_____

_____

_____

_____

_____

_____

_____

_____

_____

Becoming your own flame:

Motivation and what is it all about? Is motivation permanent? The answer is "NO." Motivation cannot live on without your participation. In other words, motivation must be motivated every day, just like taking a bath. You need to bathe every day, or you will start to **STINK**.

If your life was a movie and people were watching up to this point. What would the audience be screaming at the screen telling you to do with your LIFE.

Demotivation is everywhere. We live in a world today that talks more about our limitations, rather than our accomplishments. This often leans toward negativity and pessimism. That's why motivation is so powerful, it is the *why* behind our actions. Motivation fuels the behaviors that drive us toward our goals and dreams, and it shapes the results we experience. Sometimes those results are positive, sometimes negative. But the choice, ultimately, is yours.

Motivation itself comes from many forces' biological, social, emotional, and cognitive. At its core, it's defined as *"the reason for action; that which gives purpose and direction to behavior."* In other words, it's the spark that moves us forward.

The sources of motivation are countless: quenching your thirst, satisfying hunger, reading to expand your mind, studying to pass an exam, striving to exceed quotas at work, chasing a promotion, breaking free from addiction, or simply learning to love yourself more deeply. Each action is fueled by a reason, and those reasons shape our behavior.

Psychologist Albert Bandura defined **self-efficacy** as the belief in one's ability to succeed in specific situations or accomplish a task. That belief whether strong or weak shapes how we approach goals, tasks, and obstacles. Self-efficacy is what helps us face challenges with confidence instead of fear.

But belief alone is not enough. To harness motivation fully, you must practice two key components: **persistence** and **consistency.**

- *Persistence* means continuing to push toward your goals, even when obstacles appear.

- *Consistence* means showing up again and again, unshaken, until your efforts bear fruit.

Think about it: whether your goal is earning more money, winning a promotion, becoming a more loving person, breaking free from addiction, or simply improving yourself, none of it happens overnight. It happens because you persist through the struggle and remain consistent in the effort.

True motivation comes from within. It isn't about impressing others, it's about personal satisfaction, growth, and the pride in knowing you're becoming better than you were yesterday. Along the way, you'll discover things about yourself you never imagined possible.

Here's my perspective: everyone, at times, acts from extrinsic motivations rewards, recognition, pressure. But the more life I live, the clearer it becomes that the deepest, most lasting motivation is internal. It's the quiet but powerful act of comparing yourself only to yourself. Asking: *Am I better today than I was yesterday? Did I give more, learn more, become more?*

So, I'll ask you: are you staying motivated and striving to get better, or are you allowing yourself to grow bitter? Only you can answer that.

Right now, you should feel empowered to pursue every goal, every dream, every task you've set for yourself. Take that next action step. Lean into the challenge. And most importantly get inspired. Can I get a "Fair enough."

Notes:

_____

_____

_____

_____

_____

_____

_____

_____

_____

_____

_____

_____

_____

_____

The spark that starts within:

In a quiet village nestled between two great mountains lived an old potter named Mario. His hands were cracked from years of molding clay, yet his eyes burned with the calm fire of someone who had learned to see beauty in imperfection.

Every morning, Mario would sit in front of his spinning wheel and shape lumps of earth into vessels of bowls, jars, cups, and vases. He worked in silence, for he believed clay spoke more truth than words ever could. One day, a young traveler named Mia stumbled upon his shop. She had lost her way, both on the mountain path and in her life. Her dreams, once bold and bright, had been drowned by failure.

"Mario," she said softly, "I used to believe I was meant for something great. But the world has broken me. Every time I tried, I fell. Every time I hoped, I failed. How do you keep creating after being shaped by so much loss?"

Mario paused, wiped his hands, and pointed to a cracked pot resting on a high shelf. It shimmered strangely, as if light itself was dancing through the fractures. "That pot," he said, "was once my greatest failure. It broke in the fire. I almost threw it away. But instead, I filled the cracks with gold. Now it holds lighter than any other piece I've made." He took the broken, golden-lined pot down and placed it in Mia's hands. "Inspiration doesn't come from what goes right. It comes from what survives the fire. You were not meant to remain unscarred you were meant to shine through your scars."

Tears filled Mia's eyes. For the first time, she saw her failures not as endings, but as beginnings. She left that day not as a wanderer, but as a woman reborn with purpose ready to turn her own cracks into gold.

Moral of the Story:

True inspiration is not found in perfection, but in perseverance. The fire that breaks you can also be the same fire that refines you. Your cracks are not your weakness they are where your light gets in.

So, let me ask you this: **What inspires you?** What is the force that compels you to rise above yesterday's version of yourself and step into something greater? Because the answer to that question may just be the beginning of your transformation. Remember you can't see the picture if you are in the frame. Can I get a "Fair enough."

<u>Notes:</u>

_____

_____

_____

_____

_____

_____

_____

_____

_____

_____

_____

Rising in the face of resistance:

Growing up in a cramped one-bedroom apartment in Palo Alto with my mom, older brother, and younger sister wasn't easy. Privacy didn't exist, you could hear everything everyone was doing. My mom worked the graveyard shift, so her days were spent sleeping until it was time to wake up and head back to work, stuck in the same draining routine. Money was tight, and there was no room in the budget for preschool. Instead, she tried to teach us when she could.

But teaching wasn't her gift. I can still hear her voice tired, impatient, snapping at me when I struggle with reading or spelling. "Listen, stupid! I don't have time, so pay attention." Her words cut deep. Maybe you know someone like that someone who has no patience, no tolerance. Or maybe you've even been that way toward yourself, beating yourself down instead of building yourself up.

That's how I felt as if I was the tail, always lagging behind, always the punchline, always invisible. Just barely scraping by under the radar.

It turns out when you're in a dark place and you don't tell anybody about it. It gets darker. That's sort of how it goes so, when you're lost and you simply tell somebody, I'm lost. They're willing to just hold your hand and make you not feel alone even though the journey is still your own. It wasn't until a friend of mine confronted me and said there's something wrong and you are not telling me. I came clean. It lifted a huge weight off my shoulders, cause now, I do not feel alone in my pursuit of being lost. Because when you're lost and you keep it to yourself, and you stay LOST.

Then one day, everything shifted. I was watching TV and saw a man who seemed almost superhuman Bruce Lee. He did things with his body I didn't think were possible. In that moment, I had my first role model. Can you remember yours?

That first person who lit a fire inside you? For me, it was Bruce Lee. Don't speak negatively about yourself even as a joke. Your body does not know the difference. Words are not just sounds they are energy. Shaping the very foundation of your reality. The way you speak about yourself becomes a blueprint of how you live. Call yourself weak and weakness takes root. Speak of your strength and you begin to embody it. Think about this every I can't every I'm not good enough is seed of doubt planted in your mind. Over time these seeds grow into walls that trap you. But you have the power to plant something different Replace doubt with belief; replace I'm failing with I'm learning. Your words have the power either build the person aspires to be or shatter them, so choose wisely. Speak strength, speak resilience, speak greatness. Because the story you tell yourself today shapes the life you will live tomorrow. Remember, you were made to lead you are the head, not the tail.

Once upon a time, there was a farmer in a small village who decided to plant a grove of Chinese bamboo trees. He had heard stories about how strong and tall they could grow taller than any other plant in his field and he dreamed of seeing them sway proudly in the wind.

So, on the first day of spring, he carefully dug small holes, planted the bamboo seeds, covered them with soil, and watered them with care. Then he waited.

Days passed. Weeks turned into months. But nothing broke through the soil. Not even a tiny sprout. The farmer's neighbors watched and laughed. "You're wasting your time," they said. "Plant something that actually grows." But the farmer had faith. Every morning, he woke up before sunrise, walked to his field, watered the same spots, and tended to the invisible seeds beneath the dirt. He believed that something was happening, even if he couldn't see it. A year passed still nothing. The second year came still nothing. By the third year, many would have given up. The farmer did not. He kept watering. The fourth year arrived the field looked the same as it did on the day he planted the seeds. Then, in the fifth year, something extraordinary happened.

Almost overnight, tiny green shoots broke through the soil. And within just five weeks, those shoots shot up more than ninety feet into the air. What had seemed like years of failure suddenly became a miracle of growth. But the truth is, the bamboo hadn't been doing anything in all those years. Beneath the surface, it had been developing a strong and complex root system deep and wide enough to support its sudden and enormous growth. If the farmer had stopped watering even once, those roots would have died before ever having the chance to reveal their strength.

Moral of the story:

The story of the Chinese bamboo tree is a powerful reminder that true growth often happens underground in the quiet, unseen places of life. It teaches us patience, persistence, and faith. Just because we can't see progress doesn't mean it isn't happening. In life, just like the bamboo, our dreams, recovery, or personal transformation might take years to break through the surface. But when they do, they can grow stronger and higher than we ever imagined all because we never stopped nurturing them when no one else believed they could grow. Can I get "Fair enough."

Notes:

_____

_____

_____

_____

_____

_____

W.H.Y:

What is your *WHY*? What gets you out of bed in the morning, even when the world feels heavy and the day ahead seems impossible? I'm not asking about superficial answers your *WHY* lives deep in your heart. It's the force that drives your decisions, shapes your goals, and defines the voice only you can express. When you understand your *WHY*, you gain clarity on your dreams, your talents, your gifts, and your true purpose. Believing in yourself becomes more than an idea, it becomes a lifeline, a compass pointing you toward your best life.

Time is relentless. It is a double-edged sword, slicing through our lives whether we use it wisely or let it slip away. Too often, we waste precious hours, letting fear and hesitation hold us back. Fear is unavoidable, but you must learn to distinguish between *being afraid* and *letting fear have you*. You are your most powerful resource in confronting the obstacles that stand in your path. The ability to persist, to keep moving, and to maintain faith in yourself is what separates those who dream from those who achieve. Acknowledge your fears, face them head-on, and act anyway. What you resist will persist; what you confront becomes powerless over you.

W is for Willingness. Willingness to act, even when the weight of the world presses on you. Willingness to rise above those who doubt you or drain your energy. Willingness to confront your emotional struggles, to challenge the negative self-talk that whispers *you can't*, and to refuse stagnation. Willingness is commitment in action to keep moving forward when the easiest choice would be to give up. Surround yourself with mentors, absorb knowledge from those who have walked the path before you, and transform that insight into momentum. **Read, reflect, and apply ten pages a day of wisdom that propels you closer to your dreams.** Protect your mind from negativity, because what you feed your mind determines the height you can reach.

H is for Honesty. Radical honesty with yourself and with those around you is essential. Life will test you: you will face hurt, setbacks, and people who resent your growth. Honesty means acknowledging that you are capable of more than you've ever shown. It means taking responsibility for your thoughts and emotions, refusing to let them paralyze you. Change begins with seeing yourself clearly and choosing to act differently than yesterday. Your life is not a reflection of chance, it reflects your perception, your choices, and your willingness to interrupt the negative story playing in your mind.

Y is for You. It begins with you, and it always begins with you. You hold the power to inspire yourself and others. You are capable of more than you allow yourself to believe. You alone can nurture your dreams, your goals, your talents, and your gifts. Devote time and energy to your growth each day. Learn to love yourself fiercely, like no other. Remind yourself daily: *I am strong. I am capable. I am worthy.*

Setbacks will come, and they will feel personal, but they are not. They are lessons, not judgments. Build yourself up consistently, because if you don't, no one else will. Surround yourself with eagles.

Your *WHY* is the fire that fuels every step of your journey. Willingness is the action that moves you forward. Honesty is the lens that reveals your potential. And you are the vessel through which your dreams take shape. Embrace this truth fully, every single day. Face your fears, harness your time, and commit to becoming more than you were yesterday.

A lot of us will never truly understand our greatness, our purpose in life. Sometimes we spend all our time trying to make other people's dreams and goals come true, and we can't do that for ourselves. WHY? You don't want to wake up one day, look in the mirror and ask yourself where the time go? That is a lonely place, so take charge of your life today and cut out the emotional vampires who drain you and your dreams and your time.

Notes:

_____

_____

_____

_____

_____

_____

_____

_____

_____

Learning to walk in your new skin:

I've made it my life's mission to be a lifelong learner to sharpen my skills, refine my abilities, cultivate my gifts, and strengthen my voice. Growth isn't accidental; it requires conscious effort. When we neglect to expand our minds, we are, in essence, choosing stagnation. Choosing not to grow is slowly choosing to regress.

Growth is not optional, it is a necessity, a requirement for life itself. It is the process that transforms potential into achievement, dreams into reality, and self-doubt into self-mastery. But make no mistake: growth is not a walk in the park. It demands commitment, discipline, and the courage to face yourself honestly.

Tell yourself: *I'm starting to like myself. I will silence the negative thoughts that diminish my worth. I will recognize my value and explore my talents fully.* This is the mindset of growth. It is a conscious decision to invest in yourself, to pursue mastery over your abilities, and to honor the gifts you've been given.

Two monks were walking through a small town one was 25 years old, the other 57. The dirt road was filled with puddles from the rain the night before. As they continued their walk, a carriage stopped beside one of the puddles. A young woman stepped out, dressed beautifully, looking scared, because there was no way for her to cross without soaking her shoes and gown.

Without hesitation, the older monk walked over, turned his back to her, and said, "Climb on." He carried her safely across to dry ground. As soon as they reached the other side, the woman quickly stepped down, brushed herself off, and snapped, "Get away from me!"

The monks continued their journey in silence. An hour later, the younger monk finally spoke. "Why did you let that woman speak to you like that? Why didn't you say anything?"

The older monk smiled gently and replied, "I set her down an hour ago why are you still carrying her?"

Moral of the story:

When we hold on to the actions or words of others, we allow them to live rent-free in our minds. Judgment turns into rumination, and rumination breeds intrusive thoughts. True peace comes from letting go of doing the right thing not for recognition, but because it's who you are. Integrity is doing what's right, even when it's hard, even when no one is watching.

So, how do you want to live your life carrying the weight of others, or walking free with integrity and peace?

Understanding the urgency to act and embracing a growth mindset gives you direction. It provides a goal to aim for, a path to follow, and the momentum to move forward. Growth is not simply about learning; it is about becoming. Every step, every lesson, every challenge is a brushstroke in the masterpiece of your life. Can I get a "Fair enough."

Getting up at 5 a.m. every day to challenge your body, your mind, and yes, even your soul is not easy. Growth doesn't come from comfort. I push myself to become more than I was yesterday because I refuse to waste any more time. I don't want to wake up one day filled with regret, wishing I had gone back to school eight years ago, wishing I had started chasing my dreams sooner.

There comes a point in life when you say to yourself: *I'm sick and tired of being sick and tired. I need to do more with my life. I was made for more than this. I was designed for greatness. I am the head, not the tail.* That is growth in its raw, unfiltered form. And yes, it's difficult, because it forces you to confront your past, your mistakes, and your fears, all in service of creating a better future.

Growth is changing. Change excites us and terrifies us at the same time. We long for it yet resist it. We hope for it yet fear it. But the truth is, change is inevitable nobody stays three years old forever, and life moves with or without our permission. People come and go, moments pass, and days are lost if we don't seize them. The sooner we accept the things we cannot control, the sooner we can focus on the things we *can do* our thoughts, our choices, and our actions.

Purpose: Turn emotion into understanding. How it works: Each night, write about your day using the 3 R's:

- Reflect – What happened?
- Reveal – What did I feel or learn?
- Reframe – How can I see this differently tomorrow?

This transforms journaling from venting into emotional growth it teaches the brain to find patterns, not just problems. Learning to trust that process can be liberating, free and release it to the universe.

How it works: Instead of chasing massive change, commit to one small daily act that reflects the person you want to become reading for 10 minutes, taking a short walk, or saying one kind thing to yourself each morning. Small acts compound into identity shifts. Growth becomes a lifestyle, not a project. How will you invest the next 10 minutes to move closer to your goals?

Notes:

_____

_____

_____

_____

_____

_____

_____

_____

_____

_____

_____

_____

_____

Your thoughts create your world:

There once was a young man named James who lived in a small town surrounded by mountains. Every morning, he woke up with a heavy feeling in his chest not because of anything that was happening outside of him, but because of what was happening inside his mind. His thoughts were like storm clouds. "I'll never be good enough." "Nothing ever works out for me." "Why even try?" He carried those thoughts everywhere to work, to the store, to bed. They became the lens through which he saw everything. And slowly, they began to shape his world. His job felt harder. His friends seemed distant. His dreams, the ones he once talked about with bright eyes, now felt foolish.

One day, an old man who lived at the edge of town saw James sitting alone on a park bench, his shoulders slumped, staring at the ground. The man sat beside him quietly for a moment and then said, "You look like someone who's been fighting invisible demons." James gave a half-smile. "Yeah. My thoughts. But I can't control them." The old man nodded slowly. "Let me tell you something. Your thoughts are like seeds. Whatever you plant in your mind will grow in your life. The problem isn't that you have weeds it's that you keep watering them." James frowned. "So, what should I do?" The man picked up two small stones and placed them in James's hand. "One stone is every negative thought that tells you what you can't do. The other is every positive thought that reminds you of who you are. Every day, you get to choose which one you throw into the water. And whichever one you throw that's the one that creates ripples in your life."

That night, James went home and couldn't sleep. He thought about all the ripples he had created with his fears, doubts, and self-criticism. The next morning, he decided to do something different. When his mind whispered, "You can't," he answered, "Maybe I can." When it said, "You'll fail," he replied, "At least I'll learn." And when it tried to remind him of his past mistakes, he said, "That's where I grew roots." Day by day, his thoughts began to change not because the world got easier, but because his mind got stronger.

Weeks later, James returned to that same park bench. The old man wasn't there, but the lesson remained. He smiled, looked out at the water, and tossed a small stone the one that said, "I believe in myself." The ripples spread wide and far, just like his new way of thinking.

Moral of the Story:

Your thoughts are the architects of your destiny. They can build prisons or open doorways. Whatever you feed your mind hope or fear, gratitude or doubt will shape the life you live. Guard your thoughts, nurture them with kindness, and watch how your world transforms from the inside out. That's why it is crucial to stand up to your "itty-bitty shitty committee" that internal voice that undermines your confidence.

Think of it this way: when you go to the movies and laugh or cry, it's not because something was in the popcorn or the seats it's because of what was put on the screen. The images and stories influence your emotions, your thoughts, and your responses. In the same way, what you allow into your mind daily shapes your life, your performance, and ultimately, the person you become mind where you processed that information in your mind and started to cry or laugh? Can I get a "Fair enough."

We all perceive the world differently, and our worldview is shaped by the delicate interplay between our thoughts and our emotions. Take something as simple as a kitten, for example. Some people see the kitten and feel an overwhelming sense of love. That feeling may move them to take the kitten home, even if they don't have the time, space, or resources to care for it properly. Others may smile, appreciate the kitten, and pause to consider the responsibilities involved the cost, the time, the effort.

This simple scenario illustrates an important principle: our emotions often influence our decisions, sometimes leading us into choices that aren't in our best interest.

That's where the STAR pattern comes in a practical tool to help process thoughts and emotions before reacting. STAR stands for **Stop, Think, Assess, Respond**. By using this framework, we can prevent impulsive decisions that may lead to emotional, financial, or interpersonal challenges.

Stop. The first step is to pause and identify the thought that has captured your attention. Often, we are hyper-focused on a single thought and allow it to dominate our emotional state. For example, someone might say, *"I feel betrayed."* But betrayal isn't actually a feeling, it's an event or action. The true emotions are sadness, anger, or hurt, triggered by the thought of being betrayed. By labeling your emotions accurately, you gain clarity and prevent your feelings from hijacking your behavior.

Think. The next step is reflection. Emotions in themselves are neutral, they simply exist. But thoughts carry judgments and interpretations that can intensify your feelings. By examining the thought behind your emotion, you can identify distortions or misperceptions that might otherwise lead to reactive behavior. Are you overgeneralizing? Are you assigning blame unfairly? This step allows you to recognize how your thinking influences your emotional response.

Assess. After identifying the thought and corresponding emotion, evaluate the situation realistically. Ask yourself: *Is there an actual threat here? Is this feeling justified based on the facts?* For instance, if you feel afraid, acknowledge the fear, then determine whether there is a real danger to your safety. If not, focus on managing the feeling so it doesn't control your behavior or mood. Assessment creates space between your emotions and your actions, giving you the power to respond thoughtfully rather than react impulsively.

Respond. The final step is responding in a deliberate and healthy way. Rather than letting emotions dictate your choices, you respond with intention, guided by clarity and reason. This is where growth happens, where mindfulness intersects with personal responsibility, and where you truly begin to stand in your power.

Our thoughts shape our emotions, and our emotions influence our actions. By applying the STAR pattern, you give yourself the time and structure to process experiences thoughtfully, make better decisions, and invest in yourself. You learn to navigate life without letting impulse or raw emotion dictate your path. You learn to be mindful, intentional, and, ultimately, stronger.

Next time you are faced with something that you are having a difficult time making a healthy choice on, take the necessary time to implement the STAR pattern. You will get more than you think about this exercise.

Notes:

_____

_____

_____

_____

_____

_____

_____

_____

_____

_____

_____

_____

_____

_____

_____

_____

The war inside the mirror:

Stop it. Just stop it. It's time to silence that inner critic once and for all. The next time you catch yourself listening to that voice telling you out loud or in your mind that you're awful, no good, a loser, a liar, a manipulator, or even a monster remember this: the past does not define your future unless you choose to live there.

You were created for greatness. How do I know? Let me tell you. Out of 6.8 billion people on this planet, there is no one else exactly like you. No one has your fingerprints, your footprints, your unique combination of experiences, talents, and gifts. You are one of a kind. Your potential is unmatched.

It's time to stop believing the lies your mind tells you. Stop letting yesterday's mistakes or someone else's words shape who you are today. You are not the sum of your failures; you are the product of your choices, your actions, and your courage to rise above. Step into that truth. Stand tall. You were made for more than surviving you were made to thrive.

Can I get a "Fair enough." That is the same as your unique voice. Your voice, your thoughts, intentions, and words have the power to shape your mindset. And when your mindset changes, the game changes.

Mindset is how you see the world: the lens through which you interpret events, shape expectations, and make decisions. It is not what happens to you, but how you respond that determines your path.

There's a story about a small monastery high in the mountains of Asia. Eight young monks lived there under the guidance of a Master Monk who had been practicing inner peace for over eighty years. For the past five years, he had been training these monks, not only in discipline but in the art of cultivating the mind.

One morning, the Master Monk told the eight monks they would focus on changing their mindset but first, they had a task. They were to climb the mountain and feed the elusive blue sheep that roamed the peaks. The monks knew these sheep never stayed in one place, making the task challenging. The Master suggested they split into two groups of four: one would go up the right side of the mountain, the other the left.

To the right-side group, he placed twenty pounds of food and water on each monk's shoulders and instructed them to hurry back. To the left-side group, he placed thirty pounds on each monk ten pounds more but whispered words of encouragement: how proud he was, how honored he felt to teach them inner peace, and how blessed they were to be kind and loving to the Earth. Both groups set off at the same time.

Forty minutes later, the left-side monks, carrying the heavier load, returned radiant and joyful. They reported that the path had felt peaceful, that the sheep had come to them, and they had not struggled to find them. Twenty-five minutes later, the right-side monks returned ten pounds lighter but showing no more enthusiasm than when they had left.

The Master gathered all eight monks and asked, "What did you learn from your session on mindset?" Confused, the monks replied, "We just fed the sheep."

Moral of the story:

The Master smiled and explained: "Your lesson began the moment you left to feed the sheep. Both groups had a burden and were told to hurry. But one group received an extra weight and a whisper that went straight into their minds. That whisper shifted their mindset. It framed their challenge not as a burden, but as an opportunity. The monks with the heavier load, paired with the right mindset, finished faster and happier."

He said the lesson was simple yet profound: *You can grow through life, or you can merely go through it.* Your mindset the story you tell yourself, the lens you choose to see life through can transform your experience. Challenges are inevitable, but how you receive and interpret them determines whether they lift you or weigh you down. Feed your mind with positivity, purpose, and courage, and even the heaviest load becomes lighter.

Learning to have a mental image that goes into our mind that can set a healthy precedent can give us a sense of purpose, vision and self-confidence. Learn to believe in one's ability to not compare ourselves to others, knowing we were meant to stand out and fly like an eagle and not play with the turkeys on the bottom. Learn to forgive yourself for your past poor choices and develop positive self-talk every minute by minute; hour by hour and day by day until you love yourself like no other. Until you can look in the mirror naked, and yes, I said naked and say, "I love you and love what I see and will celebrate the small things in life." Believing that you are not a prisoner in your mind; you are free and will never stop learning; willingness to always go

39

that extra mile, because there is no traffic. Can't see the label if you are locked in the box. Can I get a "Fair enough."

Notes:

_____

_____

_____

_____

_____

_____

_____

_____

_____

_____

_____

_____

_____

Roots that withstand the storm:

There was an old man who lived on a small farm, and his grandson would visit him from time to time. One sunny afternoon, Grandpa turned to his grandson and asked, "Would you like to go into town for some ice cream?"

The boy's eyes lit up, and he shouted, "Yes!"

Grandpa smiled and said, "Then let's take the ostrich." The grandson loved riding the ostrich whenever he came to visit. Carefully, Grandpa lifted him onto the bird's back, holding the halter as they began walking toward the town.

As they made their way along the road, a car passed by. Grandpa heard a woman's voice call out, "What a shame! That poor little boy making that old man walks in this heat."

Embarrassed, Grandpa set his grandson on the ground and handed him the halter, climbing onto the ostrich himself. A few minutes later, another car drove past. This time a man shouted, "That's wrong! Letting that little boy walks in this heat he should be ashamed!"

Feeling increasingly self-conscious, Grandpa lifted his grandson back onto the ostrich next to him. But a few minutes after that, a bus rumbled by, and the driver yelled, "That's ridiculous! All that weight on that poor ostrich they should be ashamed of themselves!"

Grandpa, overwhelmed and frustrated by all the opinions, got down and finally lifted the ostrich, carrying it on his shoulders while walking beside his grandson.

Moral of the story:

It is impossible to please everyone. Those who insist on doing so will inevitably be frustrated and worn down by life.

You are unique one of a kind in a world of 6.8 billion people. Your fingerprints, your footprints, your perspective are yours alone. You dance to your own rhythm, and you cannot lose sight of that.

If you want to change something about yourself, it cannot come from trying to satisfy everyone else it must come from within. True growth, true authenticity, begins with honoring who you are, not the expectations of the crowd. To do something that you have never done; you have to become someone you have never been. Can I get a "Fair enough."

One afternoon, young Thomas Edison came home from school with a note from his teacher to give to his mother. Nancy Edison opened the letter, sat beside her son, and began to read. As her eyes filled with tears, a warm smile spread across her face. She looked at Thomas and said, "I'm so proud of you. You're doing wonderfully in school. You work hard, you're creative, and you are my little genius." That day, Nancy decided to homeschool Thomas herself. Years later, after Nancy had passed away, Thomas was going through her belongings when he came across that very letter. Curious, he opened it and read the words for the first time. The note had not praised him at all bits declared that he was no longer welcome at school, that he was "mentally ill," and that his imagination was nothing more than wild, useless fantasy.

In that moment, Edison realized the truth: it wasn't the school that had shaped his destiny, but his mother's unwavering belief in him.

Moral of the story:

A belief system has incredible power. Had Nancy told her son the harsh truth, the world may never have known Thomas Edison as one of history's greatest inventors. But because she chose to nurture his potential and teach him that the sky had no limits, Edison lived out that truth. Can't see the picture if you are in the frame. Can I get a "Fair enough."

Notes:

_____

_____

_____

_____

_____

_____

_____

_____

_____

_____

_____

_____

_____

Clearing the fog:

There was a man named Michael who lived with his wife, Blanca, about thirty miles outside of Portland, Oregon. They lived on a quiet hill with three dogs and no children. One day, while Michael was gathering firewood, he noticed a dog standing alone in the middle of the woods. Concerned about its safety, he walked over, checked for tags or identification, and, finding none, decided not to leave the dog behind. Gently, he lifted the dog and placed it in his truck.

When Michael got home, he showed Linda the dog. But instead of joy, Linda's face showed frustration. "Michael," she said firmly, "you need to take that dog back where you found him."

Michael tried to reason with her, but Linda was adamant. "Either the dog goes, or you go," she said. Reluctantly, Michael loaded the dog into his truck and drove back to the spot where he had found him.

The next morning, Michael returned home, only to see the dog sitting patiently in their driveway, waiting for him. Blanca appeared around the corner, exasperated. "I told you to take the dog back," she said.

Michael smiled, picked up the dog again, and drove further out this time, taking different streets and roads. But within minutes, he glanced back and saw the dog had found his way back home. Determined, Michael tried once more, driving eight miles out, calling Linda from the road. "Mama is the dog there?" he asked. Linda replied, "No... wait, I see something coming up the driveway. It's the dog!" Michael laughed, "Can you put the dog on the phone? I've lost my direction."

Moral of the story:

Having a clear sense of direction gives you purpose and clarity, even when obstacles appear. Life will present hurdles, challenges, and unexpected detours, but if you maintain a vision of where you want to go, your determination and focus will guide you through. Confidence comes from knowing your direction and even when the path seems confusing, a strong sense of purpose ensures you keep moving forward. Can I get a "Fair enough."

<u>Notes:</u>

_____

_____

_____

_____

_____

_____

_____

_____

_____

_____

_____

_____

Embracing the unseen path:

Embracing is defined as *the action or process of being received as adequate or suitable, typically to be admitted into a group.* I like to look at it this way: when we are children, we are often introduced to the idea of "living happily ever after." A fairy-tale vision of life where everything feels perfect, nothing really goes wrong, and nothing seems to matter. In those stories, happiness is blissful, castles are grand, birds sing, and children laugh.

But real life is different. In reality, a stable, even-keeled mindset is far healthier than chasing constant peaks of happiness. Ask most people what makes life meaningful, and few will mention fleeting emotions. Instead, they speak of relationships, family, freedom, experiences, intimacy, and purpose. These are the things that make life worth living.

Of course, life is not without its challenges: being laid off, losing a home, a car reprocessed, divorce, or even homelessness. Embracing these hardships is difficult, especially when we wish they had never happened. Life isn't fair. If it were, teachers would be paid a million dollars per year, and athletes would get paid in tips.

This is why embracing is so critical. Developing the habit of viewing every event, every challenge, through a positive lens instead of a negative, defeatist one, is essential. Embracing doesn't mean passivity, it means recognizing what you cannot change and focusing your energy on what you can change. It means choosing your perspective, no matter the circumstance.

There was a village perched at the edge of a vast forest. The villagers knew every tree, every path, every stone except one bridge that appeared only in the thickest fog. They called it

46

The Hidden Crossing. No one knew where it led, and most avoided it out of fear.

A young woman named Sammy had always been restless. She felt a pull in her heart a longing for something beyond the ordinary rhythm of the village. One morning, when the forest was blanketed in fog, she heard a whisper in the wind: "The path you fear is the one you must take."

She followed the sound. Step by step, the mist swallowed the familiar world behind her. Her heart pounded with fear, but she pressed forward. Then, just as she began to doubt herself, the fog parted, and Sammy found herself on a narrow bridge stretching across a sparkling river she had never seen. On the other side lay a valley bursting with colors, flowers, and a sunlight so warm it felt like it was lifting her soul.

Sammy realized then: the path she had feared, the one no one could see clearly, had led her to a place more beautiful than she had ever imagined. She returned to the village to tell her story, but the villagers only shook their heads, too afraid to follow. Yet she never regretted that leap into the unknown.

Moral of the Story:

The unseen path is often the one that leads to growth, discovery, and transformation. Fear is natural, but courage is choosing to step forward even when the destination is unknown. Life's most extraordinary rewards lie where certainty ends, and trust begins. Can I get a "Fair enough."

On this page, write down 6 strengths about yourself. Then write 6 things you lack in (weakness).

Examples of **strengths**: Accepts guidance/feedback, clear thinking, confident, insightful, motivate to change and supportive family and friends.

Examples of **weakness**: lack of support, low self-esteem, negative thinking, hard time thinking clearly, lack of problems solving skills, and not staying in solution.

1.   1.

2.   2.

3.   3.

4.   4.

5.   5.

6.   6.

Good, we are going to move on to the next page, and we will visit these later in the book.

Self-Rating Anxious Scale:

Self-rating scales can be a powerful tool to help you recognize when you are slipping into the anxious state I like to call "an anxious little bunny." These scales allow you to regularly check in with yourself, gaining awareness of your thoughts, feelings, and bodily sensations. Anxiety is something we all experience with students before exams, you might feel it before a blind date, and many people feel it when giving a speech. It's a natural part of being human.

A moderate level of anxiety can actually be useful. It heightens alertness, sharpens focus, and improves performance, whether at work, school, or in other areas of life. Anxiety is, in essence, the body's way of preparing us to cope with challenges.

However, when anxiety becomes constant or disproportionately intense, it can take a serious toll on both mental and physical health. Persistent anxiety can evolve into an anxiety disorder, manifesting in many ways. Signs may include feelings of dread, overwhelming fear, panic, tension, irritability, restlessness, and constant uneasiness. Anxious individuals often worry excessively about minor issues or future events beyond their control, magnifying problems that may never come to pass.

Anxiety also has tangible physical effects. The body's fight-or-flight response can produce sweating, racing heartbeats, rapid breathing, fatigue, muscle tension, tremors, and sleep disturbances. Over time, chronic anxiety can erode your overall sense of well-being.

The good news is that much of this can be managed. By practicing mindfulness and utilizing targeted techniques to regulate your response to stress, you can decrease the intensity of anxiety rather than letting it spiral out of control. Awareness and intentional practice allow you to focus on what you *can* control, rather than exhausting yourself over what you cannot. Self-awareness, paired with consistent strategies, gives you the power to move from being an anxious little bunny to someone grounded, calm, and capable, even in the face of life's uncertainties. Can I get a "Fair enough."

Let's get started, the scales will range from 1-10.

1–2: Very Mild

Anxiety is barely noticeable at this level. Most of the time, you hardly think about it. It doesn't interfere with daily activities, and you are fully capable of navigating your day without disruption. You might notice a small, lingering tension around a single issue, but it doesn't affect your sleep, appetite, or focus. You feel calm, grounded, and able to sit still with ease.

3–4: Mild to Noticeable

At this stage, anxiety becomes more noticeable and slightly distracting. You can still function and adapt, but it occasionally interrupts your focus. Engaging deeply in a task may allow you to tune it out for a time, yet it lingers in the background. Breathing remains natural, but moments of unease are more frequent, reminding you that something is unsettled in your mind or body.

5–6: Moderate

Anxiety now becomes harder to ignore, surfacing every few minutes. You can still manage work, school, or social engagements, but it requires conscious effort to focus. Irritability and restlessness may begin to affect your interactions with others, though your appetite remains intact. You are aware of the tension in your body and may notice occasional muscle tightness or a racing heart.

7–8: Severe

At this level, anxiety is intense and persistent. Restlessness dominates your mind and body, making it difficult to relax. Physical symptoms emerge blushing, flushed face, muscle tension, stiffness, grinding of teeth, and even tears. You may experience aches, twitching, or heightened startle responses. Appetite and sleep can be affected, and your emotional state becomes increasingly fragile.

9–10: Extremely Severe/Disabling

Anxiety overwhelms your senses and significantly impairs your ability to perform daily tasks or maintain social connections. Sleep is disrupted, appetite may diminish, and your voice may tremble. Muscle spasms, unsteadiness, and heightened physiological responses dominate. Functioning in normal life becomes a struggle, as anxiety dictates your thoughts, emotions, and actions. At this stage, professional support may be necessary to regain control and stability.

Relaxation techniques:

A variety of relaxation techniques can help restore balance to your nervous system by activating the body's natural relaxation response. We all experience moments of anxiousness those times when we feel like "an anxious little bunny" but the good news is, we have the power to choose calm. The relaxation response is not about lying on the couch or sleeping; it is an active, conscious process that allows your body to release tension, quiet the mind, and focus on something positive.

Learning the fundamentals of relaxation isn't difficult, but it does require consistent practice and commitment. Ask yourself: how tired are you of feeling stressed, restless, or "sick and tired" of being sick and tired? The answer is your motivation to act.

Here are a few techniques to help reduce feelings of unease and regain a sense of calm:

- **Focus on the Present:** Ground yourself in the here and now, rather than dwelling on the past or worrying about the future.

- **Visualization:** Close your eyes and imagine a place where peace surrounds you completely. See it, hear it, and feel it until it becomes real every color, every sound, every breath reminding you that calm lives within you.

- **Soothing Music:** Surround yourself with music that lifts your spirit and quiets your mind. Let each note steady your breath, each rhythm guides your focus, and each melody reminds you that peace is always within reach.

- **Social Support:** Reach out to your network friends, family, mentors, or colleagues. Sharing your feelings and seeking support is one of the most effective ways to manage stress and anxiety.

By integrating these strategies into your daily routine, you train your mind and body to respond differently to stress. Over time, you gain control, resilience, and the ability to navigate life's challenges with a calmer, more centered presence.

Breathing

Practice deep breathing by taking full, cleansing breaths this simple yet powerful technique can transform your stress in moments. Deep breathing is easy to learn, can be practiced almost anywhere, and offers a fast, effective way to calm both your mind and body. It serves as the foundation for many other relaxation practices and can be enhanced by pairing it with soothing music, gentle stretching, or quiet reflection.

All it really takes is a few intentional minutes and a space where you can pause, breathe, and be present. Give yourself permission to take this time you are worth it. By practicing deep breathing consistently, you train your body to release tension, center your thoughts, and regain control over your emotional state, even in the midst of life's chaos.

Guided image:

Visualization is a powerful tool for easing tension, reducing stress, and lifting your mood. Guided imagery, a variation of meditation, can help calm the "anxious little bunny" inside you. This technique invites you to imagine a scene where you feel completely at peace free to release all tension, worry, and anxious thoughts.

Choose the environment that feels most comfortable and safe to you whether it's your bedroom, your couch, the floor, or even your office with the door closed. You can practice this exercise alone, with a friend, or by following an audio recording. Close your eyes, take a deep cleansing breath, and allow your worries to drift away as you bring your restful place to life in your mind.

The more vividly you imagine this scene, the more effective the practice becomes. Engage all your senses:

- **See:** Picture the warm glow of a sunset over a quiet lake, loved ones laughing nearby, your pet playing, the vibrant colors of flowers, or a clear blue sky.

- **Hear:** Notice the gentle rustling of leaves, birds singing, distant rain falling, or calming instrumental music.

- **Smell:** Breathe in the scent of pine trees, fresh grass, flowers, or any aroma that brings you comfort.

- **Feel:** eel the cool water gently kisses your feet, the warmth of sunlight embracing your skin, and a soft breeze whispering across your face a reminder that peace can be found in even the smallest moments of stillness.

- **Taste:** Imagine the sweetness of fresh fruit, the refreshment of cool water, or the comforting warmth of tea.

Guided imagery works best when you immerse yourself fully, letting your mind explore each detail. The more senses you get, the deeper your relaxation, the calmer your mind, and the more your body can release tension. Over time, visualization becomes a refuge you can return to anytime, helping you regain focus, composure, and emotional balance.

Reaching out:

Another powerful way to reset and regain balance is to take intentional time to connect with the people in your inner circle. Whenever possible, aim for a face-to-face conversation, or at the very least, a meaningful phone call.

Go beyond small talk share what's truly happening in your heart, not just on the surface. Opening in this way allows others to offer fresh perspectives, guidance, and support, while also strengthening your relationships. Genuine connection has the power to ease burdens, shift your mindset, and remind you that you are not facing life's challenges alone.

Walking:

Take a walk and truly notice the beauty and abundance that Mother Nature has provided. Walking is far more than simply moving from one place to another; it can become a mindful, meditative practice. Slow your pace, synchronize your steps with your breathing, and focus on the present moment. Let each step anchor you, bringing your attention to the sights, sounds, and smells around you. If your mind feels restless or distracted, slow down even further allow yourself to fully inhabit each moment.

Take your pet along and use this time to practice mindful breathing, lowering your heart rate and calming your nervous system. Make it a habit to check in with yourself regularly, noticing your mood and how it may influence your reactions and behavior. Walking, in this mindful way, serves as a healthy distraction from stressors and gives your mind a chance to reset.

Beyond walking, engage in activities that keep your body and mind active yoga, gym workouts, martial arts, CrossFit, or other hobbies that inspire and energize you. Even simple creative pursuits like painting, gardening, or reading can provide a positive outlet. Life is a journey with only one vehicle, your body and mind. Do you want to drive through it hitting every pothole, or navigate smoothly, mindful and prepared, avoiding unnecessary obstacles? The choice is yours, and every step you take in mindfulness brings you closer to balance and clarity.

Notes:

_____

_____

_____

_____

_____

_____

_____

_____

_____

_____

_____

_____

_____

Daily rituals of self-love:

Diamond had always been "too busy" to take up hobbies. Between work, errands, and scrolling through her phone, she told herself there was no time for painting, music, or even a simple walk in the park. One rainy afternoon, a neighbor invited her to join a small watercolor class at the community center. Hesitant, Diamond shrugged and agreed, thinking, "It's just an hour. How much could it matter?"

To her surprise, the moment she held the brush, something inside her shifted. Colors blended beneath her fingers, and for the first time in months, her mind quieted. Diamond felt joy in the rhythm of each stroke, a release from her constant planning and worry. Over time, Diamond began carving out moments each week for painting, and she noticed something remarkable: she became calmer, more patient, and even more creative at work. What had seemed like a "waste of time" became her source of energy.

Moral of the story:

Life feels full when we make time for the things that feed our soul. Hobbies aren't just leisure they are essential acts of self-care and discovery.

Hobbies are the quiet sanctuaries of the soul, places where we can retreat from the constant demands of life and rediscover ourselves. They are more than mere pastimes, they are acts of self-respect, moments where our inner world takes precedence over the outer chaos. Engaging in a hobby allows the mind to wander freely, unshackled from deadlines, expectations, and judgments. In these moments, whether we are painting, writing, gardening, or playing an instrument, we nurture creativity and curiosity, the twin forces that remind us we are alive, capable, and whole. Hobbies give us permission to slow down, to breathe deeply, and to honor our own needs without guilt.

Beyond the solace they provide, hobbies serve as invisible threads that stitch together mental and emotional well-being. They reduce stress, sharpen focus, and create a rhythm in life that feels both grounding and liberating. They also offer a gentle mirror, reflecting our passions, strengths, and growth back to us in ways work or obligation never can. In the simple act of losing ourselves in something we love, we find the truest form of self-care: a reminder that our lives are not just about productivity or achievement, but about joy, discovery, and the quiet beauty of simply being. Hobbies are the soulful investments we make in ourselves, paying dividends in resilience, happiness, and a deeper connection to the life we are living.

Hobbies:

- Acting
- Aero-modeling
- Aikido
- Amateur Astronomy
- Amateur Radio
- Arts
- Astrology
- Astronomy
- Bicycling
- Bird watching
- Blogging
- Board Games
- Boating
- Body Building
- Bok fu
- Boomerangs

- Badminton
- Baseball
- Basketball
- Beachcombing
- Beadwork
- Becoming A Child Advocate
- Belly Dancing
- Canoeing
- Car Racing
- Cave Diving
- Chess
- Cloud Watching
- Coin Collecting
- Collecting Antiques
- Collecting Artwork

- Bowling
- Boxing
- Bringing Food to The Disabled
- Building A House for Habit for Humanity
- Butterfly Watching
- Button Collecting
- Crossword-Puzzles
- Cake Decorating
- Calligraphy
- Camping
- Candle Making
- Dancing
- Darts
- Die cast Collectibles
- Digital Photography
- Dominoes
- Drawing
- Educational Courses
- Electronics
- Embroidery
- Exercise (aerobics, weights)
- Fencing
- Fishing
- Football
- Frisbee
- Gardening
- Going to movies
- Golf
- Go Kart Racing
- Guitar
- Handwriting Analysis
- Hang gliding
- Hiking
- Horse riding
- Playing music

- Collecting Music Albums
- Compose Music
- Computer activities
- Cooking
- Crafts
- Crochet
- Cross-Stitch
- Hunting
- Illusion
- Jewelry Making
- Jigsaw Puzzles
- Judo
- Juggling
- Jujitsu
- Keep A Journal
- Kenpo Karate
- Kayaking
- Kickboxing
- Kite Boarding
- Learning A Foreign Language
- Learning An Instrument
- Making Model Cars
- Meditation
- Model Ships
- Mountain Biking /Climbing
- MMA Training
- Needlepoint
- Origami
- Painting
- Paper Mache
- Parachuting
- Photography
- Piano
- Pilates
- Typing
- Treasure Hunting

- Playing team sports
- Pottery
- Quilting
- Rafting
- Reading
- Reading To the Elderly
- Rescuing Abused or Abando
  Animals
- Rock Collecting
- Rockets
- Running
- Scrapbooking
- Scuba Diving
- Sewing
- Singing In Choir
- Skateboarding
- Sketching
- Sky Diving
- Soap Making
- Soccer
- Stamp Collecting
- Swimming
- Tae kwon d
- Tang soo do
- Tennis
- Toy Collecting
- Train Collecting
- Traveling

- Volunteer
- Weight training
- Woodworking
- Working In a Soup
  Kitchen/Shelter
- Working on cars
- Wrestling
- Writing
- Writing Music
- Writing Songs
- X-games
- Yoga
- Yachting
- Zoo trips

So, let's start getting comfortable, being uncomfortable. With that said, if you don't recognize any of these hobbies, then go to the internet and research! Your mind should be like a parachute; it works better when it is open. Can I get a "Fair enough."

Notes:

_____

_____

_____

_____

_____

_____

_____

_____

_____

_____

_____

_____

When words listen back:

We know that motivation and inspiration play a critical role in achieving our goals and dreams, but true growth comes when we understand where we currently stand. It is during our low points that we feel stuck, overwhelmed, or defeated that we must summon our willpower, stay hungry, and commit to growth. As you read these words, think of your mind like a parachute: it works best when it is open. An open mind allows for learning, reflection, and true personal development.

It's easy to maintain positivity when life is smooth when work is going well, bills are paid, the car runs reliably, money is in the bank, or a promotion comes your way. But genuine growth emerges when you are knocked down emotionally, mentally, or spiritually. How you respond to adversity and how you rise from it is the true measure of your growth.

There was once a teacher named Debbie who believed in the power of words. She taught language not as rules or grammar, but as a living thing something that could build, heal, or destroy depending on how it was used. Her classroom walls were lined with quotes from poets and philosophers, but the one that hung above her desk read: "Speak as though the universe is taking notes." Her students loved her, though most didn't quite understand her strange sayings. They'd laugh when she'd pause mid-lesson and ask, "Did you hear that?" even when the room was silent. One afternoon, a boy named Chris lingered after class. He was quiet, one of those students who hid brilliance behind silence. His eyes carried the weight of someone who had already been told too many times that he wasn't enough. "Ms. Debbie," he said softly, "do you really think words listen back?" She smiled the kind of smile that reaches the eyes before the lips. "Yes," she said. "Every word you speak plants a seed. The world listens, even when it seems like it doesn't." Chris nodded politely but looked unconvinced. Days passed. The seasons have changed. Then one cold morning, Debbie didn't come to class. The students were told she'd fallen ill and needed time to recover. A hush fell over the classroom that week; even the walls seemed to miss her voice.

On the third day, Chris found himself sitting alone at his desk. He stared at the empty chair where she used to sit. For the first time, he whispered aloud, "You're the only one who ever believed I could do more." He didn't expect an answer. But something strange happened. The silence seemed to soften. The air grew warm. The echo of his own words came back to him not in sound, but in feeling. The next morning, Chris arrived early. He cleaned her desk, straightened her books, and wrote a note on the board: "Words listen back so I'll keep speaking ones that matter." Weeks later, when Ms. Debbie returned, frail but smiling, she saw the message and tears filled her eyes. She didn't erase it. She left it there for the rest of the year. Years later, when Chris became a teacher himself, he hung a small sign above his own desk. It read: "Speak gently. Words listen back."

Moral of the Story:

Every word carries a heartbeat. What we speak doesn't vanish, it echoes, shaping hearts, memories, and futures. Words are not just heard they remember. So, speak as if your words might one day return to you. Because they will.

This is why evaluating your present state, setting clear goals, and taking intentional action is crucial. Life will inevitably throw obstacles, emotional stress, and crises your way. Without a clear plan and a determined mindset, these challenges can derail your growth. But history is full of people who, despite difficulties, rediscovered themselves, redefined their purpose, and emerged stronger.

Adversity, when met with persistence and reflection, develops inner strength and inner peace. It teaches resilience, sharpens your strategies, and builds the character necessary to overcome life's hurdles. On the other hand, some, like the people allow struggles addiction, mental health challenges, low self-esteem, or a sense of powerlessness to define them, never moving past the pain or fear. The choice is yours: remain in the cycle of stagnation, letting obstacles control your story, or rise to meet your challenges, use them as a catalyst for growth, and commit to the relentless pursuit of your goals, dreams, talents, and vision. True growth begins when you take ownership of your life and refuse to let fear, shame, or self-doubt dictate your path. Remember, you can't see the picture when you are in the frame. Can I get a "Fair enough."

Let's get comfortable being uncomfortable

Notes:

_____

_____

_____

_____

_____

_____

_____

_____

_____

_____

_____

_____

_____

_____

Dancing with discomfort:

Let's begin by getting comfortable with being uncomfortable. That statement alone can feel overwhelming, and for good reasons. Most of us live within the safety of our comfort zones, resisting any step beyond what feels familiar. But true growth, transformation, and self-discovery happen when we are willing to take that step when we are willing to confront ourselves in a new light.

Dr. Daniel G. Amen, MD, talks about ANTs Automatic Negative Thoughts, also known as cognitive distortions. These are the reflexive, often unconscious thoughts that pop into your mind first, and more often than not, they are negative. These thoughts can shape your perception of yourself, your relationships, and your world.

Consider this example: You're at work and your supervisor calls you over. What is the very first thought that enters your mind? Or another scenario: You're with family, and your spouse calls, asking if you're alone. What's the immediate thought that arises?

85% are automatic negative thoughts that happen to all of us, but the key is not to ignore them or beat yourself up for having them. The key is to become aware of them, challenge them, and replace them with a more balanced and constructive perspective. By doing so, you take the first step toward working on yourself, expanding your comfort zone, and seeing your life and yourself through different, more empowering lens. Can I get a "Fair enough?"

Another way to understand cognitive distortions is through what's often called **"all-or-nothing thinking."** This is the type of mental pattern that convinces your mind that things are either entirely good or completely bad, healthy or unhealthy, black or white, leaving no room for balance or nuance.

For example, imagine you've followed your exercise plan perfectly for an entire month. You might think, *"I am the most disciplined person I know!"* But then, if you miss a single day at the gym, your mind immediately flips to the opposite extreme: *"I have no discipline at all,"* and suddenly one missed session becomes a free pass to skip multiple workouts. This rigid thinking pattern sabotages consistency and undermines progress.

Some people fall into another type of distortion called **"fortune-telling,"** where they predict the worst possible outcome without any real evidence. Examples include: *"I just had a biopsy I'm sure it's cancer,"* or *"I know my boss doesn't think I can do the job."* The mind convinces you that disaster is inevitable, even when the reality is unknown.

Another common distortion is **blaming others** for your problems while refusing to take responsibility for your own successes or failures. Toxic statements like, *"It's your fault I'm out of shape because you won't exercise with me or give me tips,"* are classic examples. Anytime you start a thought with *"it's your fault,"* you hand your power over to someone else. This victim mentality leaves you feeling powerless and stuck, unable to take control of your actions or change your behavior.

Cognitive distortions like these are sneaky, they make you believe the narrative of helplessness. The antidote is awareness: recognizing these patterns, challenging them, and taking responsibility for your own choices. Once you do, you reclaim your power to make consistent, positive changes in your life. Can I get a "Fair enough."

Here is a list of cognitive distortions, I want you to pick out two from the list below that you are willing to work on and self-monitor yourself on a consistent basis.

1. **All or nothing thinking** – You tend to see the world in extremes black or white, all or nothing. If something doesn't go perfectly, your mind interprets it as a complete failure. Minor mistakes or imperfections become magnified, leaving no room for nuance or balance. Your internal dialogue might sound like: *"He's always late," "She can never do anything right,"* or *"The entire dinner is ruined just because I burnt the rolls."* In these moments, you're thinking distorts reality, ignoring the small successes or positives that also exist. This rigid mindset keeps you trapped in frustration and dissatisfaction, preventing you from responding with patience or perspective.

2. **Guilt** – Sometimes we convince ourselves that we are responsible for things outside of our control other people's feelings, actions, or even external events. We hold the belief that anything less than perfection on our part makes us inherently flawed or inadequate. This distorted thinking can sound like: *"I should have done a better job," "If I were a better person, I'd call my wife more often,"* or *"It's my fault my husband is so unhappy."* These thoughts create unnecessary guilt and self-blame, anchoring us in feelings of inadequacy and preventing us from seeing situations objectively.

3. **Fortune Telling** – When faced with participation or presenting yourself in any way, your mind often jumps to negative assumptions and self-doubt. Thoughts may sound like: *"This isn't going to be that educational," "I know they won't like my presentation," "No one will even show up to my party,"* or *"I'm not going to get that job, I just know it."* These automatic negative predictions before any evidence exists can paralyze your confidence and prevent you from fully engaging. They feed on fear and expectation rather than reality, creating a self-fulfilling cycle of anxiety and hesitation.

4. **Jumping to conclusions** – When your spouse or significant other attempts to start a conversation, your mind may automatically jump to negative interpretations, assuming the worst even when there is no factual evidence to support these conclusions. You might read tension, judgment, or criticism into neutral words or gestures, letting your thoughts create problems that don't actually exist.

5. **Magnification** – You tend to blow your problems out of proportion while downplaying or overlooking your positive qualities and strengths. In other words, you focus excessively on the small setbacks and trivial issues, letting them dominate your perspective, while the meaningful accomplishments and traits that truly matter get ignored.

6. **Blame** – When things go wrong or don't turn out as expected, there's a tendency to place the blame on someone else rather than taking personal responsibility. Your thoughts might sound like: "He's making me angry," "She forced me into this,"

or "You always hurt my feelings." This mindset shifts accountability outward, giving others control over your emotions and reactions instead of empowering you to take charge of your own responses.

7. **Mental Filter** – You tend to zero in on a single negative detail and fixate on it, allowing it to overshadow the bigger picture. This selective focus can distort your perception of reality, making everything seem worse than it actually is. For example, even if your presentation received mostly positive feedback, one minor critical comment can dominate your thoughts, leaving you obsessed over that single point instead of appreciating the overall success.

8. **Catastrophe** – We often magnify even the smallest setbacks, transforming minor inconveniences into major catastrophes in our minds. This habit convinces us that every effort we make is destined to fail or lead to disaster. Our thoughts may sound like: "I can't handle this; it's completely unbearable," or "There's no way I can change, so why even try?" By blowing problems out of proportion, we trap ourselves in a cycle of anxiety and defeat, making it harder to take positive action.

9. **Labeling** – You attach labels to yourself or other words like "lazy," "stupid," "loser," or "jerk" as if they are absolute truths. These labels are misleading judgments that distort reality and unfairly define self-worth. By labeling in this way, we allow a single action or moment to dictate how we perceive

ourselves or someone else, undermining self-esteem and limiting the possibility for growth and change.

10. **Helpless Trap** – We fall into this trap when we view ourselves as victims of circumstances, believing we have no control over our problems or outcomes. Thoughts like, "I can't handle this," "There's nothing I can do to fix my situation," or "I'll never get out of debt," reinforce a sense of powerlessness. When we adopt this mindset, we hand over control of our lives to external forces, allowing obstacles to dictate our emotions, decisions, and future. True empowerment begins when we recognize that while challenges are real, our response to them is always within our control.

Cognitive distortions have held me back in ways I didn't always recognize at the time. These faulty thoughts often arise from negative emotions, frustration, fear, anxiety, or self-doubt and they quietly guide my decisions, usually in unhelpful directions. You will start to notice ruminating thoughts that occur which will immediately turn into intrusive thoughts. When my mind convinces me that a situation is worse than it really is, or that I am incapable, I act on those emotions instead of reality in front of me. The result is avoidance, procrastination, or self-sabotage. These distorted thought patterns have stopped me from pursuing opportunities, speaking up for myself, and taking risks toward my goals and dreams. They make small setbacks feel like catastrophic failures and keep me stuck in cycles of hesitation, guilt, and regret. By learning to recognize these distortions, I can start separating emotion from reality, respond intentionally, and move forward with clarity and purpose. At this point we should have a better understanding of our cognitive distortions and how they have **hindered** you from achieving your personal goals.

You will write how you are going to be more **mindful** and **self-aware** of Ant's or cognitive distortions. What step by step plans are going to take by **standing up to yourself, and your emotional state?**

<u>Notes:</u>

_____

_____

_____

_____

_____

_____

_____

_____

_____

_____

_____

_____

_____

_____

_____

_____

It's essential to stay mindful of this cognitive distortion and consciously work to shift negative situations into positive ones. Yes, personal growth is challenging, and working on ourselves is often uncomfortable, but with patience and persistence, you'll begin to experience more joy and fulfillment in life. Remember, never give up on yourself, you are more blessed, capable, and highly favored than you may realize. Can I get a "Fair enough."

Notes:

_____

_____

_____

_____

_____

_____

_____

_____

_____

_____

_____

_____

_____

_____

Shedding the masks:

We can all agree that feeling truly comfortable in our own skin is challenging. Learning to connect and collaborate effectively with others can be just as difficult. Equally important is learning to let go of your "laundry list" of past mistakes, grudges, or negative self-talk understanding that personal growth is a gradual process. Rome wasn't built in a day, and your transformation won't happen overnight.

The most important project you'll ever work on is yourself. Take the necessary time to rediscover who you are. This process can feel both scary and exciting as you confront your strengths and weaknesses with the ones you identified on time for acceptance page. Recognizing your inherent value empowers you to explore yourself more deeply.

With that awareness of your inner greatness, challenge yourself to write down three strengths and three weaknesses you'd like to improve. Then, apply one strength and address one weakness to pursue a passion, enhance your social skills, or expand your network in a new way. Remember: there is no such thing as a "bad day," only character-building days. By consistently applying your strengths and addressing your weaknesses, what once seemed impossible becomes possible, and you move closer to the best version of yourself. Can I get a "Fair enough."

Notes:

_____

_____

_____

_____

_____

Let's get comfortable being uncomfortable

Notes:

_____

_____

_____

_____

_____

_____

_____

_____

_____

_____

_____

_____

_____

_____

_____

_____

_____

_____

_____

The fire that belongs only to you:

For the longest time, I didn't truly know who I was. Not in the sense of being confused by my reflection, but in understanding why I thought the way I did about myself and why I wasn't expressing my voice. Finding your "voice" that unique aspect of yourself that makes everything you do distinctly *you* takes time, experimentation, and yes, it can even be fun.

Imagine twenty musicians playing the same piece perfectly, note for note, yet all sounding identical. None of them are expressing their voice. Then, imagine one musician performing the same piece with their own interpretation you recognize the music, but you also immediately know who is playing it. That is your voice. It is singular, powerful, and unmistakably yours.

Your voice has the power to elevate you your dreams, your goals, your talents. But to tap into that power, you must rewrite the story you tell yourself the inner monologue that insists your voice is weak, unwanted, or unimportant. Stand up to that voice and declare: *my voice is like no other.*

You don't have to be great to start, but you do have to start to become great. Each day, take a step toward expressing your voice because this world, this life, and all its wonders were shaped by people no smarter or stronger than you. Let your voice be heard.

Remember, only **7%** of communication comes from the words you speak. The other **38%** is shaped by your pitch, tone, and volume, and **55%** by your body language and facial expressions. Think of a smooth **FM radio DJ** calm, steady, and confident. When your tone and delivery are off, your message can lose its impact. Focus not just on *what* you say, but on *how* you say it.

When you lead with genuine emotion, your brain releases neurotransmitters like **oxytocin, serotonin, and dopamine** creating deeper human connection. Be intentional with your pauses; they allow others to process, absorb, and truly feel your message. This also allows the receiver to communicate their interpretation of what you were saying.

Fair enough? Now, let's take further practice *mirroring*: reflecting others' tone, energy, and body language to build understanding and trust.

Mirroring is the quiet art of reflection in the subtle way we connect by matching another person's tone, energy, or emotion. It isn't imitation; it's empathy in motion. When we mirror someone, we align ourselves with their rhythm, showing them without saying a word I see you, I'm with you. It's how trust begins, how tension softens, and how people feel safe enough to be real. True mirroring happens when presence replaces performance. It's not about copying gestures or repeating words; it's about tuning in to the heartbeat behind them. When you listen with your body, your tone, and your silence, something powerful unfolds the other person begins to hear themselves through you.

That's the magic of mirroring: communication that doesn't just speak but connects.

Here's how to practice:

1. Match Their Pace.
If someone speaks slowly and thoughtfully, slow down with them. If they speak quickly with energy, gently increase

your tempo. Matching rhythm creates a subconscious sense of alignment.

2. Reflect Their Tone.
Listen for emotion behind their words calm, anxious, hopeful, or sad and let your tone carry a similar emotional weight. This tells them, "I get how you feel."

3. Adjust Your Volume.
If they're speaking softly, lower your voice slightly. If they're animated and expressive, allow your voice to open up too. Volume can communicate presence, care, and respect for emotional space.

4. Use Pauses Wisely.
Mirroring isn't just about how you speak it's also about how you wait. Pausing when they pause, or allowing silence after something emotional, shows that you're tuned in, not rushing to respond.

5. Match Energy, Not Emotion.
If someone is angry or frustrated, you don't need to mirror their anger just the intensity. Stay calm but engaged. It's about meeting energy without feeding emotion. How to implement everything together as you use your radio DJ voice.

Remember to breathe yes, just breathe. When someone asks you a question, it's perfectly okay to pause, take a breath, and then respond. You might worry that it looks like you don't know the answer, but it's quite the opposite. That simple breath shows calmness, composure, and quiet confidence. Can I get a "Fair enough."

Let's get comfortable being uncomfortable

Notes:

_____

_____

_____

_____

_____

_____

_____

_____

_____

_____

_____

_____

_____

_____

_____

_____

_____

_____

The strength between storms:

Life is short each day is a miracle, and you will never get this exact day back. Think about that. How you spend your time, what you focus on, and who you allow into your life all reflect who you are. Pause and consider this before reacting. How much time are you dedicating to working on yourself improving your health, protecting your energy, and staying away from emotional vampires, naysayers, pessimists, and "Debbie Downers"?

Here's the good news: it's okay to feel overwhelmed, frustrated, or down. Why? Because today is your opportunity to learn how to discipline your mindset. By mastering your mind, you unlock true freedom. Emotions are temporary, not permanent, and growing from these experiences only makes you stronger. Everyone has faced struggles similar to yours you are never truly alone. Some days it may feel that way, but perspective matters. Ask yourself: do you surround yourself with people who understand and uplift you?

The was a father who lived on a ranch with his two sons James, 16, and Titan, 14. Their home was bustling with life: cattle, horses, chickens, pigs, and yes even a donkey. Each morning before school, the boys would help feed the animals. One afternoon, James and Titan brought their report cards home. Their father, disappointed with both sets of grades, called them over to the horse corral. "I want you two to clean this corral," he instructed before walking away. As soon as the father left, James wrinkled his nose. "This place is disgusting. It stinks. I don't want to be here." Titan nodded. "Yeah, it does stink." Thirty minutes later, the father returned and asked, "So, what did you learn?" James scowled. "I learned that you're mean and unfair. It smells

horrible here, and there's nothing but manure. I'm done."
The father turned to Titan. "Do you feel the same way?"
Titan replied, "He's right it does stink, and there's a lot of
manure. But with this much, there's got to be a horse nearby
somewhere."

Moral of the Story:

The father smiled. "Exactly. It's all about perspective." James
had focused on the smell and the mess, while Titan chose to
see the possibility hidden beneath it.

Believing in a power greater than yourself can ignite action,
helping you shift your mindset from negative to empowered.
You are not defined by your past; you are prepared by it.
Mistakes and setbacks are lessons meant to teach and
strengthen you. You have a choice: act pitiful or act
powerful. That choice is yours, and that is where your true
power lies. Remember, the past does not equal your future
unless you live there.

Let me ask you something why is the lion called the king of
the jungle? It's not the fastest that's the cheetah. It's not the
biggest, that's the elephant. It's not the strongest, that's the
rhino. It's not even the loudest that's the hyena. The lion is
king because of its mentality. Now imagine if we carried
that same mentality the mindset that says: I won't stop. I
can't stop. I will not stop. The past does not define the
future. When I speak, I declare to the world exactly who I
am. This is my new mentality. I am more than a conqueror. I
am the head, not the tail.

I remember one Sunday afternoon in Portland, Oregon, after
a weekend of nonstop rain. I was teaching a workshop for

Kenpo Karate school owners, and nothing was going right. Getting people to participate was a challenge, and every little frustration felt personal. I carried this mood all the way to the airport as I headed back to San Jose, California, still letting the weekend's mishaps dictate my emotional state.

Once the plane took off, I looked out the window and noticed something remarkable: the storm covered only a small part of Portland. Beyond that, the city was bathed in sunlight. It hit me just like that storm, our problems often seem much bigger and more overwhelming than they truly are. Most of the time, the storm is limited, and the sun is still shining if we just look for it.

The good news is we are not chained to our current thoughts; we can build our ability to think differently and change that mindset and having that understanding this too shall pass. Changing your mindset will help you face and overcome diversity, hard times and difficult times. The reality is no matter how well things are, even if you have money in the bank; children are doing good in school; car is running great, and you are killing it at work this thing called life will show up! Why, I don't know why, however you will be prepared and can adapt to any mindset to fit any challenge, barrier, obstacle, hurdle, and struggle. The bottom line is if you are willing to change and compromise your current mindset, in turn that change will influence your behavior and you will focus on the positive rather than the negative events. Taking a moment to stay present will change that negative frame of mind into piece of mind. Remember, you can't see the picture if you are in the frame. Can I get a "Fair enough."

Let's get comfortable being uncomfortable

Notes:

_____

_____

_____

_____

_____

_____

_____

_____

_____

_____

_____

_____

_____

_____

_____

_____

_____

_____

_____

_____

Live Now:

See, anyone *can* but the real question is, *will you?* We are all investing our time, energy, and focusing on someone's plan. The key question is: whose plan are you investing in?

You are the director of your own movie. It can be a blockbuster or a flop. If you want it to be a hit, it starts with you. Embrace the process, enjoy the journey, and grow through it, not just go through it!

It's essential to engage in yourself and spend quality time on *you*. This movie you are making is called Life, and if you want it to be a smash hit, you need to soar like an eagle. Don't get caught playing with the turkeys, the bottom is already overcrowded. Can I get a "Fair enough."

You are creating your own production; you are the star of your life. You will come across judge-aroo's and jerk-a-saurus' and that is ok, just remember, our job is not to let a five-minute problem turn into a five-hour, five-day, five-month, or even five-year problem.

I was truly blessed to care for my 94-year-old Grandpa Craig. One of my favorite things was picking Burger King for him a Whopper with no onions, fries, and a coke with no ice and then sitting with him in his cozy mobile home, listening to his incredible stories at the dinner table. Grandpa Craig had a love for exploring pawn shops around Reno, NV, searching for used Rolex watches that had once belonged to famous gangsters needing quick cash. After acquiring a watch, he would do a sharp suit and wear it proudly, impressing at his job interviews at the *Reno Gazette-Journal*. His lifelong dream was to become a world-class journalist, chronicling Reno's growth into the "Biggest Little City" and helping to put it on the map.

Outside of work, Grandpa Craig dedicated himself to his community, volunteering at a nearby church setting up chairs for morning mass and preparing coffee and cookies for parishioners. Over the years, he shared countless stories that left a lasting impact on me.

In the late '90s, Grandpa Craig was diagnosed with Parkinson's, and three years later he developed pneumonia. One morning, I visited him and called out, "Grandpa, Grandpa, it's me, Chris. I love you, and I can't wait for you to come home so we can get your Whopper with no onions, fries, and Coke no ice. I love hearing all your stories."

Slowly, Grandpa Craig turned his head and said, "I love you like you were my own son, and I have to tell…"

The love and connection in that moment is something I will carry with me forever.

I was just a janitor at work, not the journalist I had dreamed of becoming. I spent my days daydreaming, imagining what it could have been, but fear of failure kept me from pursuing it. Instead, I settled to be a janitor and worked at the church, while much of the money I earned went gambling. Grandpa

Craig looked at me with a kind smile and said, "The best advice I can give you is this: live now. Don't die before you die. Live now."

Here's another way to look at life: imagine that tomorrow, every person you love exists only as a photograph just a memory frozen in time. What would you want to say to them today, right now, while they are still here and not a photograph yet?

That day, I told Grandpa Craig, "It doesn't matter that you didn't chase those other jobs or that you gambled. In my eyes, you're still my hero, and I'm so proud to take care of you and hear your stories over and over again." I promised him, "I'll see you tomorrow I want to hear another story."

The next day, my schedule was packed, so I planned to visit the following morning. When I arrived at the hospital, I rushed to his room, only to find it empty. Confused, I asked a nurse, "Where is my grandpa?" She wasn't sure and went to check. A few minutes later, the doctor approached me with a solemn expression. "I'm sorry," he said. "He passed this morning."

Your happiness isn't something you stumble upon, it's a state of mind you choose to allow. When you leave prejudice and sorrow behind, you breathe again, and somehow, you become unstoppable. The hidden treasure has always been inside your heart; your soul yearns to believe, to desire, and even though pain and disappointment have played their part, God gave your life because He knew you were strong enough to live it.

What does this mean? It means we must act and stay focused on solutions. In life you either are going to meet it, to beat it or you will eat it. The choice is yours. It's been always your choice.

Develop your plan, because it begins with you. Only you hold the power to take the necessary steps to move forward, to cultivate a mindset that says, "I can't be stopped, I won't be stopped, until I win, until I achieve my dreams, my goals, and find my voice." Stay hungry, stay driven, and you will reach your destination. To achieve something you've never done before, you must become someone you've never been. You can't see the full picture while you're stuck inside the frame so step out. Can't read the label if you're locked in the box. Remember: it's up to you only you can make it happen. Real change begins when the pain of staying the same is greater than the pain making the change. Can I get a "Fair enough."

Let's begin.

<u>Notes:</u>

_____

_____

_____

_____

_____

_____

_____

_____

_____

_____

_____

Let's get comfortable being uncomfortable

Notes:

_____

_____

_____

_____

_____

_____

_____

_____

_____

_____

_____

_____

_____

_____

_____

_____

_____

_____

_____

_____

_____

About the Author:

Chris Packham is a martial artist with over 32 years of experience, holding a 5th-degree black belt in the American Kenpo Karate Association, a 2nd-degree black belt in American Kenpo Karate Systems. A retired professional kickboxer who competed at the Tokyo Dome in Japan, he has led workshops across 30 states and contributed to self-defense initiatives.

Mr. Packham is also a Clinical Director and Counselor at New Life Recovery Centers, as well as Director of a substance abuse facility (LAADC, MSW, M-RAS, CADTP IV FAC). He authored the psycho-educational book *Wake Them Up They'll Listen to You!* and has been featured on CreaTV sharing insights on recovery, wellness, and martial arts philosophy.

Contact: **apathtorecovery.cp@gmail.com**

www.ingramcontent.com/pod-product-compliance
Lightning Source LLC
Chambersburg PA
CBHW060440090426
42733CB00011B/2345

*9 7 8 1 6 1 1 7 0 3 3 3 7 *